The NCTE High School Literature Series

■ ■

The NCTE High School Literature Series offers classroom teachers in-depth studies of individual writers. Grounded in theory, each volume focuses on a single author and features excerpts from the writer's works, biographical information, and samples of professional literary criticism. Rich in opportunities for classroom discussion and writing assignments that teachers can adapt to their own literature curriculum, each book also offers many examples of student writing.

Volumes in the Series

Nikki Giovanni in the Classroom: "The same ol danger but a brand new pleasure" (1999), Carol Jago

Alice Walker in the Classroom: "Living by the Word" (2000), Carol Jago

Sandra Cisneros in the Classroom: "Do not forget to reach" (2002), Carol Jago

Raymond Carver in the Classroom: "A Small, Good Thing" (2005), Susanne Rubenstein

Amy Tan in the Classroom: "The art of invisible strength" (2005), Renée H. Shea and Deborah L. Wilchek

Langston Hughes in the Classroom: "Do Nothin' till You Hear from Me" (2006), Carmaletta M. Williams

Judith Ortiz Cofer in the Classroom

A Woman in Front of the Sun

The NCTE High School Literature Series

Carol Jago

Santa Monica High School, Santa Monica, California

NATIONAL COUNCIL OF TEACHERS OF ENGLISH
1111 W. KENYON ROAD, URBANA, ILLINOIS 61801-1096

Staff Editor: Bonny Graham
Interior Design: Jenny Jensen Greenleaf
Cover Design: Jenny Jensen Greenleaf and Tom Jaczak
Cover Photo: Sortino

NCTE Stock Number: 25359
ISSN 1525-5786

It is the policy of NCTE in its journals and other publications to provide a forum for the open discussion of ideas concerning the content and the teaching of English and the language arts. Publicity accorded to any particular point of view does not imply endorsement by the Executive Committee, the Board of Directors, or the membership at large, except in announcements of policy, where such endorsement is clearly specified.

Every effort has been made to provide current URLs and e-mail addresses, but because of the rapidly changing nature of the Web, some sites and addresses may no longer be accessible.

Library of Congress Cataloging-in-Publication Data
Jago, Carol, 1951–
    Judith Ortiz Cofer in the classroom : a woman in front of the sun / Carol Jago.
        p. cm. — (NCTE high school literature series)
    Includes bibliographical references.
    ISBN-13: 978-0-8141-2535-9 (pbk.)
    1. Ortiz Cofer, Judith, 1952—Study and teaching (Secondary) 2. Hispanic American women in literature—Study and teaching (Secondary) 3. Hispanic Americans in literature—Study and teaching (Secondary) I. Title.
    PS3565.R7737Z73 2006
    818'.5403—dc22
                                                                    2006018145

Culture is our garden, and we may neglect it, trample on it, or we may choose to cultivate it. In America we are dealing with varieties we have imported, grafted, cross-pollinated. I can only hope the experts who say that the land is replenished in this way are right. It is the ongoing American experiment, and it has to take root in the class-room first.

—Judith Ortiz Cofer

If we are imprisoned in ourselves, books provide us with the means of escape. If we have run too far away from ourselves, books show us the way back.

—Holbrook Jackson

Permission Acknowledgments

■ ■

"My Grandfather's Hat" reprinted from *The Bilingual Review*, 17.2 (1992) with permission of Bilingual Press/Editorial Bilingüe, Hispanic Research Center, Arizona State University.

"Call Me María" published with permission from Orchard Press, an imprint of Scholastic, Inc.

"Women Who Love Angels" reprinted from *The Latin Deli: Prose and Poetry* by Judith Ortiz Cofer © 1993, with permission from The University of Georgia Press.

Writing rubric published with permission of Santa Monica High School, Santa Monica, California.

"An Interview with Judith Ortiz Cofer: Attempting Perfection." Renée H. Shea and Judith Ortiz Cofer retain copyright to their portions of this interview. A version of this interview was previously published in *MacComère* 7 (2005), pp. 18–31.

Contents

Listen in as Renée Shea interviews Judith Ortiz Cofer about her work and life as a writer.

Pursue further resources for information about Judith Ortiz Cofer; see also a chronology of her life and work at the end of the book.

Introduction

■ ■

For many of us, coming of age is a long, long process. Maybe that is why I am such an avid reader of Judith Ortiz Cofer. Her characters remind me not only of what it was like to be a teenager grappling with the competing demands of home and self, but also what it means to "come of age" at any age. Rich in concrete images from her Puerto Rican heritage, Cofer's work speaks to students of all ethnicities: Russian, Israeli, Persian, Salvadoran, Polish, Mexican, Nigerian, Santa Monican. How she manages to do this is partly the mystery of art, but I hope the pages that follow will help you help your students mine Cofer's texts for insight into this literature as well as for insight into themselves.

Including the works of new authors like Cofer into the language arts curriculum has become increasingly difficult. Everywhere the cry for higher test scores and improved student achievement drives instruction. But what if including work by Judith Ortiz Cofer (and Nikki Giovanni, Alice Walker, Sandra Cisneros, Amy Tan) engaged your students in such deep reading and writing that their scores went through the roof? Suggesting that reading multicultural literature is at odds with skill development is a false dichotomy. No need to choose between Mark Twain and Amy Tan or Will Shakespeare and Gary Soto; students need both. Of course, to make this happen students must read a great deal more than they currently do. We have to steel ourselves in this regard, demanding much more from all our students.

A 2005 survey by Achieve, Inc. found that as many as 40 percent of the nation's high school graduates say they are inadequately prepared to deal with the demands of employment and postsecondary education. The research indicates that preparation gaps cut across a range of core skill and knowledge areas—most notably "work habits, ability to read and understand complicated materials, and writing skills" (21). Nearly 65 percent of students in college report that they wish they had applied themselves more in middle and high school. Eighty-one percent of recent graduates say they would have worked harder if their school experience had demanded more of them. It is also possible that they would have worked harder if the curriculum had included more multicultural literature. I don't believe that the inclusion of writers of color in the curriculum is a panacea for closing the achievement gap, but it can be an important feature of course work that both ensures that students meet state standards and invites them to explore engaging contemporary literature.

Anyone who works with teenagers knows that convincing students to work hard in middle and high school is a challenge. Students should be working in Vygotsky's zone of proximal development (ZPD), in which instruction is conducted at the level where students can learn with the aid of a teacher or knowledgeable peers (Vygotsky). In too many cases, middle and high school instruction is not operating in this ZPD but rather in the ZME, a zone of minimal effort. In this instructional zone, the texts are as short as possible; every day's lesson stands alone to eliminate reliance on students doing homework reading; and basic skills are retaught ad nauseam. While I understand the reasons teachers find themselves working in this zone of minimal effort, under such conditions students' hearts and minds are dangerously shortchanged.

Teachers can take heart from Achieve's findings to reaffirm our commitment to offering students a rich curriculum full of both classic and contemporary texts that push students outside the zone of minimal effort. When choosing books for students, I first look for literary merit. Without this, the novel or poem will not stand up to close scrutiny or be worth the investment of classroom time. Texts that work best for whole-class study

- are written in language that is perfectly suited to the author's purpose
- expose readers to complex human dilemmas
- include compelling, disconcerting characters
- explore universal themes that combine different periods and cultures
- challenge readers to reexamine their beliefs
- tell a good story, with places for laughing and places for crying

Judith Ortiz Cofer's work meets every one of these criteria. Her stories, like all good literature, deepen our experience, heighten our sensibilities, and mature our judgment. I believe that teenagers want to have these experiences, but many have not yet realized that books can provide them.

Reading is not a vaccine for small-mindedness, but it does make it difficult to think only of oneself or one's own ethnic group. You may not have a single Puerto Rican student in your school, yet Judith Ortiz Cofer's characters will teach teenagers of any culture more about themselves and about others. If one purpose of education is to prepare students for the complex responsibilities of citizenship, I can think of no better preparation for these responsibilities than reading rich, multicultural literature. It is not a matter of matching percentages of books to the percentages of ethnic groups in your school; it is about broadening young people's horizons. In *Poetic Justice*, Martha Nussbaum writes about her experience as a visiting professor in law and literature at the University of Chicago Law School. The university had determined that for these future attorneys and future judges to be fully prepared for the work that lay ahead, they needed to educate their imaginations. Richard Wright's *Native Son* was required reading. Nussbaum argues, "If we do not cultivate the imagination in this way, we lose, I believe, an essential bridge to social justice. If we give up on 'fancy,' we give up on ourselves" (xviii).

There is no simple fix for closing the achievement gap. This is not to say there is nothing teachers can do to narrow it. We must treat every moment of classroom time as golden and ensure that the curriculum is full of rich, engaging literature. The gap may not be closed in my lifetime, but with determined effort by parents, legislators, administrators, teachers, and students, we can work toward ensuring that the next generation leaves school with an education that has prepared them well for life. The alternative is a perfect storm.

1 Where Life and Art Intersect

In many ways, Judith Ortiz Cofer has always lived in two worlds. Born in Puerto Rico in 1952 to a father in the U.S. Navy and his young Puerto Rican bride, Cofer's early years were spent shuttling between Puerto Rico and Paterson, New Jersey, where her father was stationed. While her mother was keen that Judith should know and love her island heritage, her father wanted his children to have more choices than he felt were open to him as a young man. The tension between these two forces informs much of Cofer's work. In *Woman in Front of the Sun*, Cofer describes this experience:

> In the 1960s, growing up in two confusing and increasingly fragmented cultures, I absorbed literature, both the spoken *cuentos* I heard the women in my family tell and the books I buried my head in as if I were a creature who consumed paper and ink for sustenance. (108)

Educated primarily in public schools in the United States, Cofer moved while in high school to Georgia, where she later graduated in English from Augusta College.

> As a young college student I first majored in sociology, hoping to find a way to change the world. With the Vietnam War on my TV screen daily and the other ongoing attacks on my po-

litical naiveté, it was not long before the spell of innocence was broken. For the spiritual sustenance I craved I returned to my first love, literature. Although the world was tearing itself asunder, each author I read put it back together for me, giving order to chaos, however fleetingly. (109)

Cofer went on to earn a master's degree in English at Florida Atlantic University. During this time, she attended a graduate summer program at Oxford University. In an essay from *The Latin Deli*, Cofer describes the stereotypes she was forced to confront as a Latino woman:

> On a bus trip to London from Oxford University where I was earning some graduate credits one summer, a young man, obviously fresh from a pub, spotted me and as if struck by inspiration went down on his knees in the aisle. With both hands over his heart he broke into an Irish tenor's rendition of "Maria" from *West Side Story*. My politely amused fellow passengers gave his lovely voice the round of gentle applause it deserved. Though I was not quite as amused, I managed my version of an English smile: no show of teeth, no extreme contortions of the facial muscles—I was at this time of my life practicing reserve and cool. Oh, that British control, how I coveted it. But "Maria" had followed me to London, reminding me of a prime fact of my life: you can leave the island, master the English language, and travel as far as you can, but if you are a Latina, especially one like me who so obviously belongs to Rita Moreno's gene pool, the island travels with you. (148)

The cultural schizophrenia Cofer experienced as a child in New Jersey, where the family spoke Spanish at home, ate Puerto Rican food, and practiced strict Catholicism, was with her still. During her first year in graduate school, Cofer's father died in a car accident. Though much was left unspoken between them, he continued to direct her goals through his own unfulfilled dreams.

He was an intellectual who did not go to college, a dreamer without hope, an artist without a medium. So I went to college. I became a teacher and later a writer. I had to finish what he had never even begun at the time of his death. My mother could not bear life in the States without him as her interpreter and companion, so she went home to her Island. She got what she always wanted, but not in the way she wanted. She wanted a return to *la Isla*; she got it, but without him. I stayed behind with my books, my memories. (*Woman in Front of the Sun*, 22)

Rather than reject either side of her inheritance, Cofer embraces the richness of both worlds. Currently teaching at the University of Georgia in Athens where she is Franklin Professor of English and Creative Writing, Cofer was awarded the PEN/ Martha Albrand Special Citation in nonfiction for *Silent Dancing: A Partial Remembrance of a Puerto Rican Childhood* (1990), the Anisfield-Wolf Book Award for *The Latin Deli* (1993), the Paterson Poetry Prize for *The Year of Our Revolution: New and Selected Stories and Poems* (1998), and, most recently, the Américas Book Award for her novel *The Meaning of Consuelo* (2003).

Cofer is often asked why she writes in English rather than Spanish. She explains:

My choice of language is not a political statement: English is my literary language, the language I learned in the schools of the country where my parents brought me to live as a child. Spanish is my familial language, the tongue I speak with my blood relatives, that I dream in, that lies between the lines of my English sentences. (*Woman in Front of the Sun*, 106)

A poet, essayist, and novelist, Cofer lives in Georgia with her husband, John Cofer, and has one grown daughter, Tanya, a mathematician.

Call Me María

In Judith Ortiz Cofer's novel *Call Me María*, Cofer offers young readers a narrator whose life mirrors many of our students' lives, if not in particular, certainly in essence. Cofer's fictional María left Puerto Rico and her schoolteacher mother to live in a New York basement with her father, the building superintendent. Readers see New York City through María's eyes as she watches from a sidewalk-level window, reading the unfamiliar populace from the knees down. María is torn between two worlds—the rich island life she knows and loves and the tough environment of New York City, where she must struggle to express herself in another language. While she longs for the warmth of home, she knows how much her father needs her: "At times, he seems to be angry with me, but I know it is not me he sees when he is yelling at me for little things. I know that he is afraid I will leave him too like he knows Mami will" (31).

The novel is composed of poems, prose, and letters to María's distant mother.

Call Me María
Judith Ortiz Cofer

It is a warm day, and even in this *barrio*
the autumn sun feels like a kiss, *un besito*,
on my head. Today I feel
like an iguana seeking a warm rock
in the sun. I am sitting
on the top step of the cement stairwell
leading into our basement apartment
in a city just waking
from a deep and dark winter sleep.
The sun has warmed the concrete,
rays falling on me like a warm shower.
It is a beautiful day

even in this barrio, and today
I am almost not unhappy.
I am a different María,
no longer the María Alegre
who was born on a tropical island,
and who lived with two parents
in a house near the sea
until a few months ago,
nor like the María Triste, the lonely
barrio girl of my new American life.
I am fifteen years old.
Call me María.

Sometimes,
when I feel like a bird
soaring above all that is ugly or sad,
I am María Alegre.
Other times,
when I am like I will never
see the sun again,
I am María Triste.
My mother used to call me
her *paloma*, her dove,
when I was *alegre*,
and her *ratoncita*,
her little mouse,
on the days when I was *triste*.
Today I am neither.
You can just call me María (1–2)

After we read "Call Me María," I ask students to make a list of how the world outside looks to them when they are happy, in an upbeat mood, and feeling good about their lives. I remind them to show details—sunshine reflecting off passing cars like fireworks, scrumptious rocky road ice cream, poppies blooming—rather than "telling" with vague generalizations. Students then list descriptions of how that same scene appears when they are feeling blue. Does everyone seem to be wearing black? What is the sky like? Are babies crying? Horns honking? Sirens blaring? I draw symbols for the five senses (sight, sound, taste, touch, and smell) on the board and ask students to include on their lists details that would trigger at least four of the five senses in a reader (see Figure 1.1).

Once students begin to see how images help a writer convey tone, I ask them to put themselves in a setting they know well. This could be the view from their bedroom window, a favorite spot in the park, the seat they always choose on the bus, a place where they have often camped, the backseat of their mom's car—anyplace they have been on multiple occasions. I then have students take a piece of notebook paper and fold it in half. On the left-hand side, they describe what they see from this vantage point when they are in a positive frame of mind. On the right, I have

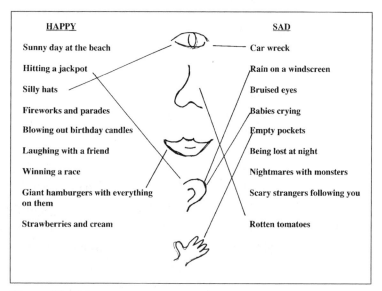

Figure 1.1. Using sensory imagery.

them describe the same scene when they are feeling blue or un-happy. I invite them to work on both sides of the fold. No need to finish one before starting the other. When their pieces are complete, students title them with their names: "Call Me Will," "Call Me Natasha," "Call Me Maria."

This lesson has been adapted from a prompt in John Gardner's *The Art of Fiction: Notes on Craft for Young Writers*. Gardner has his students describe a single landscape from the point of view of three different characters. Adapting and adjusting, borrowing and bending are what good teachers do. I hardly ever read a description of a lesson that I don't end up fiddling with to match my own classroom style or particular students. I hope you do the same with the ideas presented in this book. The next time I use these lessons I am likely to do things a bit differently myself! What doesn't change is my objective in having students do this kind of personal writing. I believe that just as Judith Ortiz Cofer has used writing to come to understand herself, so can my students. Not all of their work will be published, but all of it, when honestly written, is important. Writing is a tool for self-discovery. It lends permanence to our experience and helps us understand who we are.

I know that I am a better teacher for having written so much about my classroom. For thirteen years, I wrote an education column for various newspapers and in that time learned to take whatever was happening, good or bad, and reflect on it at the keyboard. Problems become interesting dilemmas worthy of scrutiny. I don't always come up with solutions but find in the act of writing a way of making peace with troubling circumstances. Judith Ortiz Cofer has written extensively about her own experiences as a writer. She explains in gorgeous detail how she has taken the seeds of her Puerto Rican heritage and grown them in American soil. The fruit that her poems and stories bear will nourish readers for a long time to come.

2 Writing Poetry from Models

Most students love to write poetry. Though they may moan and insist that they don't know how when you assign them to write a poem, expressing themselves in verse comes naturally to many young people. Through song lyrics, our students have extensive experience with the form. They can often recite hundreds of lines from memory and know in their bones, even if they are yet unable to articulate why, a strong phrase or image from a weak one. What makes their own poems so remarkable is their instinctive candor. Emily Dickinson said to "Tell all the Truth but tell it slant." My students seem to do this naturally.

The difficulty, of course, is getting started. How does a poet choose a subject, write that first line, select a form, develop an image, and bring the poem to a satisfying end? Edgar Allan Poe was annoyed that many thought the creation of a poem was a happy accident or simple work of genius. In his experience, writing poetry was hard work. Excellent poems required careful thought and planning. In 1846, Poe penned an essay titled "The Philosophy of Composition" describing the process he employed when writing "The Raven": "It is my design to render it manifest that no one point in its composition is referable either to accident or intuition—that the work proceeded step by step, to its completion with the precision and rigid consequence of a mathematical problem" (164). Poe explains that he began by considering the effect he wanted to achieve. His decision to focus on the universal exploration of Beauty lost led him to make subsequent decisions regarding the poem's subject, length, tone, diction, narrative arc, refrain, and theme. Poe's first choice of a bird to voice the refrain "Nevermore" had been a parrot, but this "was superseded forthwith by a Raven, as equally capable of speech, and infinitely more in keeping with the intended tone" (166).

It is important for students to understand that good poetry rarely just happens. Producing quality work requires careful attention to the craft of writing. In *Craft Lessons*, Ralph Fletcher and JoAnne Portalupi describe craft as the cauldron in which the writing is forged. An artful teacher suggests ingredients and helps students stir with thoughtful intention. While this process may not be as precisely circumscribed as the one Edgar Allan Poe employed, it depends on perspiration every bit as much as inspiration.

Women Who Love Angels

Judith Ortiz Cofer explains her process of creation:

> My books are neither Puerto Rican emigrant history nor sociological case studies; at least, I didn't write them as such. I tell stories that recount the suffering and joy of the Puerto Rican emigrants of my experience, mainly women; I re-envision the scenes of my youth and transform them through my imagination, attempting to synthesize the collective yearnings of these souls into a collage that means Puerto Rican to me, that gives shape to my individual vision. (*Woman in Front of the Sun*, 114)

Cofer goes on to say that if the poems and stories she has conjured up out of memory add up to a universal message, "then I consider myself fortunate to have accomplished much more than

I allow myself to hope for when I sit down in front of that blank sheet of paper that calls to my restless spirit like a believer's candle" (*Woman in Front of the Sun* 115). While blank sheets of paper do not call to my students the way they call to Cofer, the young men and women I teach certainly have restless spirits. Writing poetry can be a way to channel that energy and help them explore their own experiences, lending them value and meaning by giving them expression.

"Women Who Love Angels" is a poem of Cofer's that I was drawn to and wanted to share with my students. The poem appears in her collection *The Latin Deli: Telling the Lives of Barrio Women*. Although I had no idea before I began this lesson just how powerful this short text could be, I had an inkling that the poem might have instructional potential both as a text for practicing our interpretive skills and as a model. Following such hunches is one of the things I love best about teaching. Often I hear complaints that standards and standardized testing are draining the creativity out of classrooms. That only happens when we let it. As long as teachers are cognizant of what students need to know and be able to do and design lessons that are carefully constructed to help students meet those standards, students will perform well on state assessments. Every one of the tenth-grade students who participated in this lesson on "Women Who Love Angels" passed our state's exit exam. Teachers who love students know that standards-based instruction comes in many shapes and forms.

Women Who Love Angels
Judith Ortiz Cofer

They are thin
and rarely marry, living out

their long lives in spacious rooms, French doors
giving view to formal gardens
where aromatic flowers
grow in profusion.
They play their pianos
in the late afternoon
tilting their heads
at a gracious angle
as if listening
to notes pitched above
the human range.
Age makes them translucent;
each palpitation of their hearts
visible at temple or neck.
When they die, it's in their sleep,
Their spirits shaking gently loose
from a hostess too well bred
to protest.

Before initiating a class discussion, I wanted my tenth graders to do some preliminary thinking about the poem. I handed out copies of "Women Who Love Angels," read the poem aloud, and then asked students to write for eight minutes about their first impressions. I told them that if they ran out of ideas to write about they should reread the poem and choose one line that struck them to reflect on. After scribbling a paragraph that he subsequently crossed out, speculating that Cofer was "talking about the kind of person she would like to be. . . . She might be describing either what she feels an angel would be like," Henry Garf reread the poem, started again, and wrote, "I think Cofer might be referring to women who are above everyone else. They have no worries. They just get everything handed to them and everything is perfect and peaceful. But it seems as though they *know* they are so ahead of everyone. They love angels. How can you love angels? It might be they love something that you can't really love."

This is exactly the kind of thinking that freewriting is meant to foster. In his first crossed-out paragraph, Henry wrote himself into an indefensible interpretive hole. After rereading the poem, he had a different, more thoughtful and more accurate, understanding, which led to further questions. If instead of writing his way through the poem Henry had simply offered his first interpretation to the class in open discussion, a teacher would be tempted to steer him in another direction. This experience might have reinforced for Henry that he doesn't "get" poetry and should avoid taking interpretive chances. Instead, he took the time and accepted the invitation to reconsider his initial idea in light of the words on the page. It wasn't the teacher but the poem that encouraged him to make the corrections.

Ruth Campos had a similar experience. Her first crossed-out paragraph that was all about angels was labeled "Did not get it at 1st!" Ruth went on to write, "These women have great precious lives that everyone envies. They have everything, money is not an issue. They think they are better than everyone else. Supposedly everything they do they do it graciously and perfectly. They even get to die in their sleep. They get to have a great death unlike many other people" (see Figure 2.1). The freewriting allowed us to begin our discussion at a deeper level without my—as the teacher—having to nod vaguely at students' initial responses and then ask directive questions. If the purpose of literary study is the creation of readers who both can and do read literature, teachers should structure lessons in ways that build student confidence in their own ability to read. It isn't enough to rely on the two or three students with their hands raised who already know how to interpret poetry.

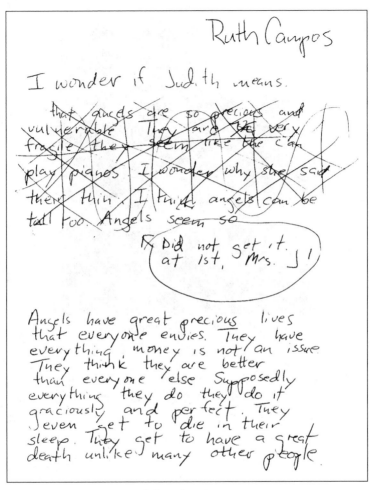

Figure 2.1. Having second thoughts about a poem.

Unsure of her English, Qiuxue Tan is one of those students who rarely speak up in class. How unfortunate it would have been for me not to know what she saw on her own in Cofer's poem: "I wonder if there are actual people like this? This kind of woman mostly appears on TV, books, and our imagination. They

Ruth Campos is thinking about angels.

are the figures whom all women look up to and want to be. Everyone would want to be always peaceful like these women. Cofer probably wrote this to show that even the most "perfect" women cannot be truly happy. They isolate themselves from other humans in order to seem angelic." Teachers can develop the confidence of young readers by taking them through a series of instructional steps that allow them to figure things out for themselves. A pattern I often use is:

1. Read a short text aloud to the class.
2. Have students read the text silently and write for five to eight minutes.

3. Have students share their thinking (not necessarily their writing) with a partner.
4. Ask who has learned something about the poem from his or her partner.
5. Use these responses as a springboard to full class discussion.

When I opened up the conversation about "Women Who Love Angels" to the whole class, we talked for the rest of the period about

- why these women are thin and rarely marry (asexual? infertile? childless?)

- the difference between formal and wild gardens with weeds

- the kind of music they play on their pianos and how it would be different if these women were strumming a guitar or beating out a rhythm on drums

- what it means to be thin-skinned, how they survive if not by toughness

- how it is that they can slip away to death so painlessly

- why angels

No prefabricated list of teacher questions could ever have been as successful at instigating such powerful responses to the poem. Throughout the discussion, it was important for me to make sure students saw that our interpretations were all based on specific images in the poem. Students were clearly "recognizing and understanding the significance of various literary devices, including figurative language, imagery, and symbolism and explaining their appeal" (California English Language Arts Reading Standard 3.7). Critics of standards-based instruction sometimes forget that well-written language arts standards describe best practices. Addressing this tenth-grade standard wasn't a distortion of what I wanted students to learn for the day. It was my goal.

Toward the end of our discussion, I urged students to consider how the poem would be different if Cofer had written about women who love tigers. Too many students believe that interpreting literature requires a gene—one they don't think they possess. I teach them to look at an image, consider what they already know about that image (e.g., pianos or thinness or angels), and use what they know to make sense of the poem. It isn't nearly as difficult as students think it is going to be.

Students Who Love Poetry

To deepen students' understanding of Judith Ortiz Cofer's craft, the following day in class I invite them to write their own poems modeled after "Women Who Love Angels." If asked to articulate how this poetry-writing exercise is standards-based and prepares students for higher education and the workplace, I have only to point to the American Diploma Project benchmarks for writing, which prescribe that students should "interpret significant works from various forms of literature: poetry, novel, biography, short story, essay, and dramatic literature; [and] use understanding of genre characteristics to make deeper and subtler interpretations of the meaning of the text" (37). Many students who struggle with interpretation have limited understanding of how a poem works. As they imitate Judith Cofer's methods, young writers not only create something new of their own but also begin to comprehend the original poem at a "deeper and subtler" level.

We began by brainstorming on the board possible subjects for our poems. Students offered:

- surfers who love waves

- readers who love the Gossip Girls series

- men who love the remote

- vegetarians who love McDonald's

- girls who love to laugh

I offered a form for them to employ as a template but urged students to deviate from it however it suited their purposes. Rather than making copies of this template that encourages a fill-in-the-blanks approach to the assignment (see Figure 2.2), I make a transparency of the form and project it on the board. I also suggest that students refer to Cofer's poem for ideas whenever they get stuck.

What took me by surprise was the extent to which students wrote about themselves, revealing aspects of their inner lives that are seldom given space in school assignments. I was stunned by their willingness to write about their secret selves—their hopes, their fears—and amazed by the power of Judith Ortiz Cofer's poem to inspire such work. Tyler Martin, a young man much addicted to computer games, wrote:

Guys Who Love Video Games

They are overweight, nerdy,
and seldom ever have money,
living their days on the couch
or chair, conquering every game
in their library: Max Payne,
Psychomauts, Pikmin, Vexx,
Halo, Resident Evil, Half-Life.
They play straight through games—

_____ Who Love _____

They are _____
and _____
_____.
They _____
in the _____
_____
_____
_____
as if _____
_____
_____.
_____makes them _____
_____
_____.
When they_____ , it's _____
Their spirits _____
_____
_____

Figure 2.2. Poetry writing exercise template.

eight, ten, or twenty hours—
their bodies so in tune with the game
that there is no need for sleep.
They wait in long lines for new games,
their hearts pounding when the first
person in the queue is let through.
When they die, it will be with controller in hand,
buried with their Gamecube,
Xbox, PS2, or last console.

It is said that when death takes the spirit
of a gamer, their soul possesses
any wireless controller that another
avid fledgling video game player owns.
                              —*Tyler William Martin*

I cannot help but think that Tyler's poem is a cautionary tale, warning himself of the dangers in store unless he learns to control his own penchant for video games. The only help I gave Tyler as he was writing was to suggest including the specific names of the video games, as concrete images communicate more powerfully than generic terms. Tyler has not been the most dutiful of students and, while compliant about beginning assignments, he often fails to turn in a finished product. After weeks of nagging him about a late term paper that I knew he had done the research

Tyler Martin composes on the computer.

for, I had to settle for a reflective essay describing the process he went through and the reasons he was unable to take the last steps toward completion. Tyler's poem, however, was written, revised, and printed within a single class period. He didn't have time to let procrastination or fear of failure get in the way of taking his idea to fruition.

Dylan Early, a star baseball player and natural athlete, tall and handsome but extremely shy, wrote:

Athletes Who Love the Spotlight

They are tough
and always on the job.
Hard-working and always fun to watch
they play like bulls
and are as pampered as any.
Gods on the court
and idols off,
these All-Stars are hardly ever too short.
Never losing a chance
to win that extra buck
they grow each year in fame
Getting better and better,
so no one can ever be the same.
As they move on
something is always lost.
Never to be forgotten
There is always the hall of fame.

—*Dylan Early*

Is Dylan imagining his own possible future as a professional athlete? How well this fifteen-year-old understands the pitfalls that surround the spotlight. Reluctant to stand in front of the class or read aloud, is Dylan examining his own fear of fame? He seems to be exploring the intrinsic danger of standing out.

Adrienne Beitcher examines the social context within which teenagers move. Her critique is acerbic and reveals much about her own penchant for gossip.

Girls Who Love Gossip

They are young,
like really good looking
They get entwined
in the gossip, the rumors,
the people's lives they
like don't even know
The drama
As if it were like their responsibility
to be nosy.
Knowing the latest gossip makes them
like so popular
When they hear, "Like, oh my god, did you hear
about that senior girl who is like pregnant
with some football player's baby, what a slut,"
their whole bodies buzz with excitement
eager to spread the rumor all around school tomorrow.
—*Adrienne Beitcher*

A subtext that informed "Girls Who Love Gossip" is that young women at my school are besotted with Cecily von Ziegesar's Gossip Girls series. I'm afraid I bear some responsibility for this craze, but as you can see from Adrienne's poem, these students are (mostly) critical readers and aware of the dangers of unchecked rumor. Hanna Bellini, a very beautiful blonde who does indeed love math and is also a reader of Gossip Girls, wrote:

Blondes Who Love Math

They are peppy
and try out for cheerleading
even though they take no pleasure in it.
They go on constant diets
attempting to achieve that perfect body.
In the dead of night
they take out their graphing calculators
and eat chocolate.
They only do this after they have sat in their pink canopy beds
gossiping for hours surrounded by magazines and nail polish
as if they cared about those things.
In truth they yearn for numbers
and want to explore the math world
They just want everyone to leave them alone
so they can solve equations.
They do math in secret
Their spirits fly free,
ecstatic to be doing what they love
Finally able to express their true selves
down under all that perfect blond hair.

—Hanna Bellini

When in another lesson I asked students to imitate Nobel Prize–winning poet Wislawa Szymborska's poem "Some Like Poetry," Hanna went home and wrote twenty poems using the pattern. When signing yearbooks at the end of the year, she copied several into other students' yearbooks. Qiuxue Tan, herself a violinist, wrote a poem so precious we sat in hushed amazement when, in a very small voice, she read it to the class.

Girls Who Love Dolphins

They are fragile
and seldom speak, saving

their every breath by the ocean,
white silk dresses
flowing behind them with grace
They play their violins
In the early morning
floating away
with the gentle melodies.
When they sleep, it's shallow
Deep in the night
letting their spirits
be carried gently by the wind.
—*Qiuxue Tan*

Listening and Speaking

Though every state and national standards document lists listening and speaking as critical language arts skills, almost no one

Qiuxue Tan reads her poem to the class.

assesses student progress in these areas. As a result, teaching listening and speaking is often shortchanged. I was reminded of the importance of these two "lost" language arts when my son, newly employed at a financial consulting firm, showed me his first performance evaluation. In the communications section of the rubric (see Figure 2.3), five criteria referred to listening and speaking.

You might think from these descriptors that James's job is in sales or management, but he works in internal audit. In a wide range of workplaces, our students will be judged on the basis of their ability to listen and speak.

Qiuxue, like many shy students, needed particular help learning to address her audience, look up when reading, and project her voice. We also need to teach students how to listen and respond to one another's poems. Applause isn't enough. I want students to learn to analyze one another's work just as they would

Communication	Rating (1–10)
• Conducts effective interviews and captures appropriate information	
• Verbally articulates information in an organized, concise, and logical manner	
• Practices active listening and employs mirroring techniques to ensure understanding	
• Understands others' perspectives and validates their positions	
• Demonstrates an ability to evaluate audience and tailor-written and verbal communication accordingly	

Figure 2.3. Communication criteria for a performance evaluation rubric.

Judith Ortiz Cofer's poem. Along with deepening their ability to interpret poetry, students are also practicing how to "understand others' perspectives." Before a student writer reads to the class, I assign two designated listeners. Because teenagers are familiar with the idea of designated drivers, the role makes intuitive sense to them. The designated listeners must pay particular attention during the reading and be the first to comment with a specific line from the poem that appealed to them and be prepared to explain why. These comments seed further discussion of the poem. Qiuxue's poem inspired a rich conversation on the nature of dolphins and why the idea of their communicating with humans is so compelling. What kinds of people love these creatures?

Another Judith Ortiz Cofer Poem to Imitate

We all know someone who is characterized by a particular piece of clothing or appendage. It might be an uncle with a perpetual pipe hanging from his lips or a skater dude cousin who could not be parted from his ragged Van sneakers. I asked students to think about a person—could be a friend, relative, familiar stranger, or themselves—and the object they associate with him or her. After giving them about four minutes of thinking time, I asked students to talk with a partner about this person and the object. Afterwards we read Judith Ortiz Cofer's poem "My Grandfather's Hat."

My Grandfather's Hat
In memory of Basiliso Morot Cordero
Judith Ortiz Cofer

I cannot stop thinking of that old hat
he is wearing in the grave: the last gift
of love from his wife before they fell
into the habit of silence.

Forgotten as the daughters chose
the funeral clothes, it sat
on his dresser as it always had:
old leather, aromatic of his individual self,
pliable as an old companion, ready to go
anywhere with him.

The youngest grandchild remembered
and ran after her father, who was carrying
the old man's vanilla suit—the one worn to *bodas,*
bautismos, and elections—like a lifeless
child in his arms: *No te olvides*
del sombrero de abuelo.

I had seen him hold the old hat in his lap
and caress it as he talked of the good times
and, when he walked outside, place it on his head
like a blessing.

My grandfather, who believed in God,
the Gracious Host, Proprietor of the Largest Hacienda.
May it be so. May heaven
be an island in the sun,
where a good man may wear his hat with pride,
glad that he could take it with him.

Following guidelines similar to those described for "Women Who Love Angels," Fionnan O'Connor wrote the following poem about a shirt that we all knew well from his repeated wearing of it. As you can see, he is an extraordinarily gifted young man.

My Grey Shirt

(that I have had since the eighth grade
and that is so comfortable that I have often
fallen asleep in class while wearing it)

You came to me with the age of reason
Three years ago but now you have grown old
Worn by the marks of every season
Climate, stain and feeling even
And yet, each and every day you are, however, altered by the cold,
Repaired by the very thing that tears your cotton:
The fact that you will never be forgotten
Such an old shirt never truly can go rotten.
Your value rises with every tear.

You are the rags of Beckett's Estragon and Vladimir.
You are the robes of Tyr-na-n'og's immortal Prince Madir.

You will always be inexorably tied
To the feelings and memories that live inside
My soul and mind for you are memory itself
And in all my writing you have dwelt.

You are everything that I have seen and done
The Moon, an apple, this poem, the sun.
You are every mile that I have run
With your sleeves I have often wiped my sweat
Into those sleeves I have often wept.

You are every book that I have read
And every thing that I have said
For all these things I've done in you

You are all my art to me
For you are like sweet Mnemosne
Mother of all the muses
Goddess of eternal memory

You rose up out of my closet like some long-forgotten thought
That rises up and suddenly presents itself anew
You are the grey and tattered shirt that I have worn
In every dream that I have had since I was two.

Your texture is like a blanket
So soft that een in the daytime I may return to sleep
Lapsing into the subconscious deep
Where all my memories flow back to me
And sing through my mind in harmony
With a melody of dreams composed of odes to thee.
—*Fionnan O'Connor*

Imitation isn't a cheap way to an easy poem. It is an invitation to authentic expression. As students follow in Judith Ortiz Cofer's footsteps, they learn her craft.

3 Reading at Risk

■■■■■■■■■■■■■■■■■■■■■■■■■■■■■■■■■

In June 2004, the National Endowment for the Arts (NEA) issued a report that sent shivers down the spine of teachers across the nation. *Reading at Risk: A Survey of Literary Reading in America* reported that literary reading is declining rapidly, particularly among the young. Despite all the effort teachers had expended bringing young adult literature, multicultural literature, literature circles, book clubs, and "reading is fun" initiatives to students, young people still weren't developing the reading habit. What were we doing wrong? What could we do better? In his introduction to the report, Dana Gioia, a distinguished poet and critic as well as chairman of the NEA, states:

> Although the news in the report is dire, I doubt that any careful observer of contemporary American society will be greatly surprised—except perhaps by the sheer magnitude of decline. *Reading at Risk* merely documents and quantifies a huge cultural transformation that most Americans have already noted— our society's massive shift toward electronic media for entertainment and information.
>
> Reading a book requires a degree of active attention and engagement. Indeed, reading itself is a progressive skill that depends on years of education and practice. By contrast, most electronic media such as television, recordings, and radio make fewer demands on their audiences, and indeed often require no more than passive participation. Even interactive electronic

media, such as video games and the Internet, foster shorter attention spans and accelerated gratification.

While oral culture has a rich immediacy that is not to be dismissed, and electronic media offer the considerable advantages of diversity and access, print culture affords irreplaceable forms of focused attention and contemplation that make complex communications and insights possible. To lose such intellectual capability—and the many sorts of human continuity it allows—would constitute a vast cultural impoverishment. (vii)

I do not think teachers are to blame for this crisis. I do think teachers are this country's best hope for turning the tide. Advanced literacy is a specific intellectual skill and social habit. The earlier this skill is acquired and the habit established, the more likely children are to read as adults. Some researchers have suggested nine as the magic age.

Reading by Age Nine

When I was nine years old, Saturday mornings meant trips to the library. Living as my family did in an unincorporated area outside Chicago city limits, the public library was actually a storage room behind the local grammar school. The place was windowless, chairless, and bulging with books. A volunteer manned the dusty checkout desk three hours a week, fifty-two weeks a year. With no idea that libraries might look otherwise, I thought the place a paradise.

On my first visit, I went straight to the adult in charge. I hesitate to identify Mrs. Martin as a librarian, as it seems doubtful that she would have held any formal qualifications for the job other than a love for books and a fondness for children. I quickly informed her that I wanted to read all the books in the library. To the grand lady's eternal credit, Mrs. Martin didn't laugh. Pointing to shelves marked with a Dewey Decimal system "92," she suggested I start with biographies. For the next few months, I worked my way through a set of books whose titles began with *The Life of* _____. I can still recall how the end sheets of each volume depicted a time line of the person's life winding around the page. Pathologically methodical, I read the series in alphabetical order: *The Life of Amelia Earhart*, *The Life of Mamie Eisenhower*, *The Life of Leif Eriksson*. By the time I got to *The Life of Marco Polo*, it began to dawn on me that my plan to read from shelf to shelf might benefit from revision. Fortunately, Mrs. Martin had other ideas about how I could choose books.

It sounds dramatic, but this silly little library saved my life. Not that my childhood was particularly miserable or in any obvious way painful, but I simply didn't like being a child. I thought all games were stupid and all kids in the neighborhood boring. The only people I had any time for were those I met in books. I mean, who can compete with the Scarlet Pimpernel or Tom Sawyer as boon companions? Had it not been for that makeshift public library, I don't know how I would have learned how to be human. A few years later I discovered that I could apply for a Chicago Public Library card, and suddenly it seemed as though I would never be at a loss for a good book again. But though the collection in this "real" library was large and the building a clean, well-lighted place, I missed Mrs. Martin. How could I find the right book among so many?

Judith Ortiz Cofer had much the same experience as a young reader. Where I had Mrs. Martin, Cofer had Sister Rosetta:

> The next week she handed me a paper sack containing *Women in Love*, *Madame Bovary*, and *Wuthering Heights*. They were public library copies; she had actually checked out two books that I

thought might be included in the church's list of banned writings! All she said was, "Make sure you put them in the drop box by the due date."

Of course I went home and lost myself in them. D. H. Lawrence appealed to me most, with his reckless immersion into language. Flaubert was too careful and precise for my taste. (I did not yet suspect that I had begun to read a page for the effect the words had on me rather than just for the juicy parts.) But it was the storm surging within Heathcliff that transported my imagination to places I wasn't yet quite able to identify.

Sister Rosetta continued to feed me books, neither asking me what I wanted nor quizzing me on their considerable effects. Under her tutelage, I read Hawthorne, Poe, *The Odyssey*, the stories of Katherine Anne Porter, Dante, the Romantic poets, even James Joyce (whose *Ulysses* was totally impenetrable, so I gave up on it). And always there was D. H. Lawrence, my dark, mysterious man, and the Brontës, who, like me, lived on the small planet of circumstance and who spoke to me about boundaries and how a smart woman might take flight through art. All the words I did not yet possess were my source of secret torment and joy. Sister Rosetta's was a reading list without apparent order, but it all came together inside me. My vocabulary expanded, my English improved, my restlessness doubled. (*Woman in Front of the Sun*, 8–9).

Cofer insists, "Books kept me from going mad. They allowed me to imagine my circumstances as romantic: some days I was an Indian Princess living in a *zenana,* a house of women, keeping myself pure, being trained for a brilliant future. Other days I was a prisoner: Papillon, preparing myself for my great flight to freedom" (*Woman in Front of the Sun*, 67). Reading offered both Judith Ortiz Cofer and me "irreplaceable forms of focused attention and contemplation." It made "complex communications and insights"—the kind we both so hungered for—possible.

Still Reading at Nineteen

My students hunger for complex communications and insights, too, though they often don't know it. By the time they come to high school, many are reading far below grade level and will tell you for free that they hate to read. They need help feeling human. Kids worry that they are the only ones who have ever felt or thought as they are feeling or thinking. Newly discovered desires scare them. No one seems to understand. The characters in Judith Ortiz Cofer's stories offer young readers hope. All are somewhat lost and in search of answers to questions that adults have mostly stopped asking. All are sensitive and suffering the pain of a fragile person in a rough world. The following titles work well as selections for a literature circle focusing on the theme of Books That Help Teenagers Feel More Human:

- *Call Me María*, Judith Ortiz Cofer

- *The Curious Incident of the Dog in the Night-Time*, Mark Haddon

- *Ender's Shadow*, Orson Scott Card

- *Lost in Place*, Mark Salzman

- *The Meaning of Consuelo*, Judith Ortiz Cofer

- *The Member of the Wedding*, Carson McCullers

- *Monster*, Walter Dean Myers

- *A Tree Grows in Brooklyn*, Betty Smith

- *What's Eating Gilbert Grape?* Peter Hedges

You will notice that the list includes something old, something new, something borrowed, and something for boys. We need to get our students reading—a book every three weeks is my rule of thumb—because more than reading is at stake. The NEA report unambiguously demonstrates that

> readers play a more active and involved role in their communities. The decline in reading parallels a larger retreat from participation in civic and cultural life. The long-term implications of this study not only affect literature but all the arts—as well as social activities such as volunteerism, philanthropy, and even political engagement. . . . Reading is not a timeless, universal capability. Advanced literacy is a specific intellectual skill and social habit that depends on a great many educational, cultural, and economic factors. As more Americans lose this capability, our nation becomes less informed, active, and independent-minded. These are not qualities that a free, innovative, or productive society can afford to lose. (vii)

Writing Reflective Essays

Inspired by Dana Gioia's warning and the terrifying extrapolation that if trends for the dramatic increase in books published and the dramatic decrease in readership continues, in fifty years there will be exactly one reader for every book, I asked my students to reflect on Judith Ortiz Cofer's experience with reading and to compare it with their own. California's English Language Arts Standards require students to write reflective compositions that

- a. Explore the significance of personal experiences, events, conditions, or concerns by using rhetorical strategies (e.g., narration, description, exposition, persuasion).

- b. Draw comparisons between specific incidents and broader themes that illustrate the writer's important beliefs or generalizations about life.

- c. Maintain a balance in describing individual incidents and relate those incidents to more general and abstract ideas. (70)

I assigned students the following writing prompt:

Writing Situation
Judith Ortiz Cofer wrote, "Books kept me from going mad. They allowed me to imagine my circumstances as romantic: some days I was an Indian Princess living in a *zenana*, a house of women, keeping myself pure, being trained for a brilliant future. Other days I was a prisoner: Papillon, preparing myself for my great flight to freedom."

Writing Directions
Analyze the point Cofer makes about the power of reading. What role do books and reading play in your life? Use examples from the book you have just read as well as from other books you read for pleasure and for school.

I offer these excerpts partly as examples of how students responded to this prompt but also to counter claims that boys aren't reading. My students are. Grant Overmire (grade 10) wrote:

Cofer makes a very important point in very few words when she describes reading. She speaks the truth in illustrating how important reading a story is and showing the power reading has on one's imagination. The short description of various roles and characters that can be easily slipped into by just picking up a book gives a good summary of what reading is about. The power of reading yields the ability to turn to a different world and assume the role of anyone that you feel like being. From becoming the world's greatest warrior in *Beowulf*, to being just an insect on the wall in *The Metamorphosis*, authors act as gatekeepers, each one leading us down a different journey inside our own head. The styles of different authors hit the soul like different flavors of gourmet food. . . . Reading has the power to educate, entertain, and bring an experience right into your own room. I feel that reading will always have a place in my life and I will make sure that it stays important to me.

Almost a year after Grant Overmire wrote this, his mother sent me the following e-mail message: "I would like to take a moment to thank you for all you have done for my son. When Grant was little, he loved reading. In his early elementary years he read just for the fun of it. Somewhere along the line his interest in reading and writing was quashed. Your class re-ignited his interest and he blossomed. I thank you for all you have done to hone his skills. He now enjoys reading and writing again. Sincerely, Wendy Overmire." Teachers don't always know how the seeds they sow come to fruition.

Chris Pratt (grade 10) wrote:

> Why read a book rather than sitting and watching a multi-million dollar movie? Judith Ortiz Cofer stated that books kept her sane and allowed her to be whomever and whatever she wanted. Books are a personal escape, a portal to another dimension. Reading enables us to put ourselves in the situation of the main character where viewing a movie only gives the satisfaction of seeing the director's interpretation of the story. I owe much to books because they have taught and raised me, each with their own separate style and reasoning. When you watch a movie made from a book you think the way the director thinks because that is how he/she understood the reading. Literature trains our minds, whereas movies are simply for entertainment.

Sebastian Pacheco (grade 10) wrote:

> Reading allows you to take up personalities which you are not. A brave soldier, a beautiful princess, even an evil president if that is what you fancy. Cofer's statement about detaching yourself from the world is 100% true. Those with little self-confidence find shelter in books and help people of all ages escape. I think if you don't read, you'll go mad.

Chris Pratt writes about his reading.

Eliza Smith (who went on to win an NCTE award in writing) wrote:

> We read because we are human—it is in our nature to be interested in dramatic story lines, odd characters, a different era, etc., because we see ourselves in the text. . . . We look to books not for mere comfort and pleasure, but for the reflections of ourselves that we find in them.

Assessing essays that are both personal and reflective can pose tremendous challenges. How do you assign a grade to writing that is clearly explorative and probing? I don't for a minute want to suggest that the following rubric answers this question fully, but it helped bring consistency to how teachers in our English department at Santa Monica High School evaluated our tenth-grade final exam prompt that asked students to write a reflective essay:

10th grade June common assessment
Reflective Writing Prompt

Writing Situation
While thought exists, words are alive and literature becomes an escape, not from, but into, living. To what extent does literature set people free and allow them to live?

Writing Directions
Plan and write an essay in which you explain your views on this issue. Support your position with reasoning and examples taken from your reading, studies, experience, or observation.

Teachers evaluated student essays using the following reflective writing rubric.

Reflective Essay Rubric

5

IDEAS AND EXPLANATIONS—These essays explore and reflect upon the significance of personal experiences, events, or concerns and draw comparisons between specific incidents and broader themes that illustrate the writer's important beliefs or generalizations about life. They maintain a balance in describing individual incidents and relate those incidents to more general and abstract ideas.

ORGANIZATION uses appropriate transitions between and

within paragraphs for consistently clear, smooth, and logical relationships among ideas.

STYLE is a "pleasure to read"—graceful, uncluttered, rich, and vivid.

GRAMMAR and MECHANICS errors are rare or absent.

4

IDEAS AND EXPLANATIONS—These essays explore and reflect upon personal experiences, events, or concerns and draw comparisons between specific incidents and broader themes that illustrate the writer's important beliefs or generalizations about life.

ORGANIZATION is logical and appropriate for content, but may not use appropriate transitions.

STYLE is clear, shows sentence variety, and uses interesting and precise vocabulary.

GRAMMAR and MECHANICS errors are occasional.

3

IDEAS AND EXPLANATIONS—These essays explore and reflect upon the significance of personal experiences, events, or concerns.

ORGANIZATION constructs body paragraphs that relate to the thesis but is simplistic OR relationships between ideas are unclear.

STYLE is functional but sentence variety and vocabulary are limited OR style is wordy.

GRAMMAR and MECHANICS errors are frequent.

2

IDEAS AND EXPLANATIONS—These essays retell personal experiences without reflection.

ORGANIZATION shows some minor skill but has major flaws—e.g., no controlling idea; poor paragraphing; redundancy.

STYLE has major flaws—e.g., simplistic, repetitious, monotonous, often unclear.

GRAMMAR and MECHANICS errors exist in almost every sentence and interfere with meaning.

1

IDEAS AND EXPLANATIONS—These essays present few or no ideas and explanations. They may be incomprehensible OR essay is too short to judge.

ORGANIZATION lacks paragraphing, is chaotic, illogical, and/or confusing.

STYLE has such severe flaws that essay is hard to understand.

GRAMMAR and MECHANICS errors are pervasive and interfere with meaning.

I am an unapologetic lover of rubrics, yet even I was perplexed by how to assess an essay like the one below. What do you do when a student is so clearly off the charts? I assign a 5 and thank heavens for the gift of teaching students with such insight and wisdom. When I read the following essay, Molly's candor and insight left me breathless:

Dealing with Death
by Molly Strauss

Though ever present, the subject of death is often avoided by the living. However, even when ignored, it continues to take victims. My mother, Laurie, died of breast cancer when I was only 10 years old. Overwhelmed, I turned to literature as an escape. To my surprise, I discovered that instead of blocking out my pain, novels drew me into it. Exploring death in literature became therapeutic, helping me to process hidden emotions and thereby live more fully.

In *To the Lighthouse*, Virginia Woolf documents the life of a functional, average family at their vacation home over two summers. Between visits, the mother unexpectedly passes away. The turmoil that follows paired with the family's previous serenity is a perfect juxtaposition; it embodies the essence of death. Readers experience the total loss of control—the chaos—of a sudden end to life. Mrs. Ramsey held her family together, playing whatever role was required: wife, mother, and friend. In her absence, each member of the family must learn self-sufficiency, fulfilling their own needs instead of relying on Mother or Wife to do it for them. My mother's death forced me to become my own person at an early age. Like the Ramseys, I no longer had the luxury of nurturance and attention. I resented her for leaving me to fend for myself. Instead of giving me relief from these emotions by blocking them out, *To the Lighthouse* helped me understand the *beauty* of my experience. As I watched the

Ramseys learn to take care of themselves, I saw my own "tragedy" as a gift. The loss of my mother forced me to become mature, and as a result I developed into a healthier, more self-reliant person. By thinking about the Ramseys' growth as a result of death, I was able to see my life in a different light.

Emily Brontë's portrayal of death in *Wuthering Heights* shows the effects of ignored grief. When Catherine passes away, her soul mate, Heathcliff, is devastated. Over the years, he fails to deal with his emotions, instead ignoring the pain. This failure to accept death, to accept that life continues after Catherine, turns Heathcliff into a bitter, unloving old man. His transformation served as a warning for me. I realized the importance of confronting emotions head on, and now reap the benefits. Instead of hiding my grief, I cry. And as a result, I can live without the hidden baggage Heathcliff experienced.

"Stone Boy," a short story in *Points of View* by Gina Bericault, explores the repercussions of a freak accident. When a six-year-old child accidentally kills his older brother, his shock and guilt are enormous. These, in combination with his family's uncompassionate reaction, destroy the boy for life. He becomes "stony," unable to process his feelings. Guilt, though often irrational, is a lifelong disease. "Stone Boy" helped me understand that no one has complete control over life—that some events are no one's fault. I experienced guilt when my mother passed away, though I had no control over the situation. Like Stone Boy, I took responsibility for something completely out of my hands. By recognizing that the "killer" in "Stone Boy" was not to blame for his brother's death, I pronounced *myself* "not guilty."

Literature has provided me with a way to understand myself. It is impersonal; I am able to analyze death without being wrapped up in my own experiences. Novels allowed me to process my mother's passing. As a result, I can live without death ever present.

I think teachers are the luckiest people in the world to witness such wonder. I should send this essay to Dana Gioia at the NEA to give him hope. Reading may be at risk, but with the help of writers like Judith Ortiz Cofer, teachers possess the power to break the trend.

4 Teaching Literary Analysis

▪▪▪▪▪▪▪▪▪▪▪▪▪▪▪▪▪▪▪▪▪▪▪▪▪▪▪▪▪▪▪▪▪▪▪▪

What is it about first-person narration that so appeals to readers? Why are we drawn to these quirky and touching stories told from a limited point of view? Readers know they are hearing only the narrator's side of the matter and that the account is likely to be biased and unreliable. They can't witness anything the narrator chooses not to tell us. Yet instead of detracting from the power of the story, these limitations draw readers deeply into the narrator's world. Could it be that we find these stories so compelling because they allow us to be someone else?

I know that as a young reader I was always keen to be anyone other than my boring, goody-two-shoes self who helped her mom with the babies and got good grades. When I read Holden Caulfield's plaintive, "If you really want to hear about it, the first thing you'll probably want to know is where I was born, and what my lousy childhood was like, and how my parents were occupied and all before they had me, and all that David Copperfield kind of crap, but I don't feel like going into it" (Salinger 1), I was hooked. Traveling with Holden from his school full of phonies to New York City, I took chances I would never have dared take outside the covers of a book. Seeing the world through Holden's eyes helped me understand that angst was a common human condition.

Along with offering readers an escape from their own safe worlds, first-person narratives allow us to explore cultural worlds otherwise closed to us. Everything I know about what it means to grow up in a barrio or in war-torn Yugoslavia I learned from narrators who lived there. This might not be the most reliable way to learn geography or history, but for me the stories have made a lasting imprint on who I am. They have also caused me to read newspapers and history with deeper understanding. First-person perspectives may be limited, but these narrators know whereof they speak. Their stories ring true. As we read, we learn how the circumstances of the narrators' lives are different from ours, as well as the extent to which internal circumstances—alienation, loss, isolation, fear—remain constant.

Often teachers claim that the reason their students don't read well is their lack of background knowledge. After the first administration of California's exit exam, many urban teachers complained about the use of an excerpt from Jack London's *Call of the Wild*, pleading that their city-bred students knew nothing of the Alaskan wilderness. At first I took the criticism to heart. Maybe the passage was a poor choice. Then I thought again. What did I, growing up on the South Side of Chicago, know of the "wild"? Nothing. What allowed me to comprehend and connect to London's tale were all the dead dog stories I had read as a ten-year-old.

The Meaning of Consuelo

The solution to students' lack of background knowledge is not more field trips. The kind of travel that students, both urban and rural, need is textual. As young readers view the world through points of view seemingly foreign to their own, the boundaries of their world expand. Take, for example, this passage from Judith Ortiz Cofer's novel *The Meaning of Consuelo*, set in 1950s Puerto Rico:

> My island is so small it disappears on a globe or a map of the world. But as a child I could not see the end of the land from anywhere I stood, so to me it was as large as I needed my world to be. I was the daughter of a proud and troubled young man and a pretty, vivacious young woman who took pleasure in their children, but I was a *niña seria* from the start, preferring a picture book to the rowdy company of other children, story time to parties. Just like my silent brooding father. His silences were the vacuum Mami abhorred, having grown up around laughter, shouts, and angry cries—noise meant life for her. I perceived her disappointment and retreated further inward as a result. After my sister, Maria Milagros, was born when I was four, Mami finally had the cheery companion she thought a child should be. (12)

I have never been to Puerto Rico, yet Cofer takes me there. As I walk in Consuela's footsteps, I become this character. Though the surroundings are different from what I know, I too was a *niña seria*, a serious child. For 180 pages, I live in a San Juan suburb and grapple with living up to a name that means comfort and consolation. I both suffer and laugh as Consuela navigates her entry into womanhood within a culture where female self-sacrifice is taken for granted. When she declares, "I belong to myself," I cheer.

While an informational text might offer more practical data about Puerto Rico, I have a short attention span for cold detail. Within the context of this compelling first-person narrative, I begin to consider how Consuela's life parallels Puerto Rico's struggle to retain its cultural identity. I want to know more. What I read about the island now has a human context and is, as a result, comprehensible.

A question that readers often want to pose to writers who employ first-person narration is the extent to which the character is the author. J. D. Salinger spent much of his life hiding from fans intent on knowing if he was really Holden Caulfield. Judith Ortiz Cofer has been more forthcoming:

> In my books I follow memories, *cuentos*, events, and characters that I see as my guides back to what Virginia Woolf calls "moments of being" in my life, both in Puerto Rico and in the United States. It is a process of discovery. My books are neither Puerto Rican emigrant history nor sociological case studies; at least, I didn't write them as such. I tell stories that recount the suffering and joy of the Puerto Rican emigrants of my experience, mainly women; I re-envision the scenes of my youth and transform them through my imagination, attempting to synthesize the collective yearnings of these souls into a collage that means Puerto Rican to me, that gives shape to my individual vision. If these *cuento* I create out of my memory and imbue with my perceptions add up to a universal message, then I consider myself fortunate to have accomplished much more than I allow myself to hope for when I sit down in front of that blank sheet of paper that calls to my restless spirit like a believer's candle. (*Woman in Front of the Sun*, 114–15)

Cofer makes it clear that readers must not assume that just because an author chooses to write in the first person that the text is therefore autobiographical. Behind Consuelo and Holden is the controlling presence of an author wearing the character's mask. When Holden laments, "What I like best is a book that's at least funny once in a while. . . . What really knocks me out is a book that, when you're all done reading it, you wish the author that wrote it was a terrific friend of yours and you could call him up on the phone whenever you felt like it. That doesn't happen much, though" (42), was Salinger describing his own experience as a young reader? We'll never know. Fortunately, teachers do know many books that a *niña seria* like Holden would love. Quite a few have first-person narrators.

The Elements of Literature

Though the elements of literature were created equal, some are more equal than others. Take, for example, characterization. Without a main character to cause a reader to care about what happens, the plot seems a pointless series of events. Without a character's point of view to direct our sight, the most haunting setting looks like one more old house on a hill. Characters give a human face to literature and provide an entry point for readers, especially students with special needs, to experience story. Often students with special needs are acutely sensitive to being somehow "different" from everyone around them. Focusing on characters who feel themselves set apart from the crowd helps these students discover that there is a place for all of us in literature . . . and in life.

Call Me María, a novel in letters, poems, and prose, provides students with an engaging story perfect for analyzing the elements of literature. María muses on her dilemma: "It is a beautiful day / even in this barrio, and today / I am almost not unhappy. / I am a different María, / no longer the María Alegre / who was born on a tropical island, / and who lived with two parents / in a house near the sea / until a few months ago, / nor like the María Triste, the lonely / barrio girl of my new American life. / I am fifteen years old. / Call me María" (1). Who would not want to read on and learn more about this first-person narrator?

What draws readers to María is that she is so clearly a dynamic character, poised for change. In fiction we talk about flat and round characters. A flat, or two-dimensional, character is built around a single idea or quality. Often, but not always, such characters represent stereotypes. Such characters—think of Mr. Micawber in Charles Dickens's *David Copperfield*—remain essentially unchanged throughout a story. By contrast, round characters are complex. Their temperament is changeable and their motivation multifaceted. As in real life, such characters are difficult to describe in a single phrase or by a single trait. Cofer has created a round, dynamic character in María. In many ways, she reminds my students of Sandra Cisneros's Esperanza in *The House on Mango Street*. "At times, he seems to be angry with me, but I know it is not me he sees when he is yelling at me for little things. I know that he is afraid I will leave him too like he knows Mami will" (31).

Just as in real life, round characters are capable of surprising us. This does not mean, however, that they are inconsistent. A character cannot be suspicious and cunning on one page and naive on the next unless specific events account for such a change. At the same time, complex youthful characters are often in the process of maturing and will therefore—like real teenagers—behave like adults in one context and like children in another.

Authors use two distinct methods for developing characters: showing and telling. When "showing," an author presents the character talking and acting and leaves the reader to draw conclusions about motivation. The reader infers what is ticking inside characters' minds by attending to what they say and do. Such showing can also entail revealing what is going on inside a character's mind. In *Call Me María,* Judith Ortiz Cofer offers readers a window into her main character through letters María writes to her mother, through poems María writes, and through the use of a first-person narrator. Another common term for this method is *indirect characterization*.

When "telling," an author steps into the story, talking directly to the reader regarding the character. This is also known as *direct characterization*. Jane Austen does it best:

> Mr. Bennet was so odd a mixture of quick parts, sarcastic humour, reserve, and caprice, that the experience of three-an-twenty years had been insufficient to make his wife understand his character. *Her* mind was less difficult to develop. She was a woman of mean understanding, little information, and uncertain temper. (7)

In contemporary writing, such "telling" is often considered a violation of artistry, but one has only to read Nikolai Gogol's *Dead Souls* or Voltaire's *Candide* to see how in the hands of a master such authorial intervention can add another often humorous or ironic dimension to the text.

When teaching characterization, I like to have students fill in an open mind like that in Figure 4.1. Together we brainstorm character traits, and then I ask students to choose one trait to look for in the next night's homework reading. I give students sticky notes and tell them to write the trait on it and when they find an example of this trait, to mark the place in their books. The next day in class we go around the room, with each student identifying the trait they chose, reading the passage from the text, and then explaining how this quotation demonstrates their chosen character trait.

CARA: The trait I chose was "determined" and the quote is on page
    62. It says, "Today I will go downtown by myself. I will

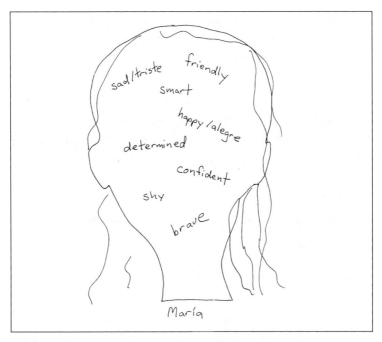

Figure 4.1. Open mind: María from *Call Me María*.

practice English with real people and try to learn more about
the world outside this block so that one day I will stop feeling
lost in the world. Maybe I can learn to think of this city as
home." I think this quote shows that María is determined
because she is putting her mind to doing something she
doesn't really want to do but knows she has to so she can stop
feeling bad about being in New York and missing Puerto Rico
so much.

The lesson becomes particularly powerful when students have
chosen the same character trait but different passages. Often when
students write character analysis papers, they describe a trait, of-

fer evidence, but fail to connect that evidence to the generalization they want to prove. This oral practice seems to help students understand what it means to explain a quotation and to analyze their evidence.

When I think of the books that live inside me, it is almost always characters that come to mind first: Esperanza in *The House on Mango Street*, Sethe in *Beloved*, Raskolnikov in *Crime and Punishment*, Scout in *To Kill a Mockingbird*. Every one of these characters has made the journey from trial to triumph. Teaching students how characterization works can be a key to unlocking comprehension as well as a door opening to a lifetime love affair with books.

5 An Interview with Judith Ortiz Cofer: Attempting Perfection

■ ■

Renée H. Shea

The following interview was conducted by Renée Shea, NCTE member, professor of English at Bowie State University in Maryland, and author of *Amy Tan in the Classroom*. Renée is a regular contributor to *Poets and Writers* magazine.

RENÉE SHEA: How did you choose the provocative title *A Story Beginning in Spanish* for your new book? Why did you decide to gather this collection of poems, many that have been published before in journals and magazines?

JUDITH ORTIZ COFER: Poetry books are usually formed that way. You publish a lot of different poems in journals and at some point you feel that you have a critical mass. The poems in this collection date back as far as fourteen years, so it's a new book in that it's newly collected work. I've always felt that a poetry book has to coalesce, come together in form, so I don't write poetry in the same way I write novels—which is with one idea in mind. I have quite a few poems that I kept looking at and wondering if they made a book, and about two or three years ago I thought a pattern was emerging, not just a thematic pattern but a way of looking at the book as a whole. I thought that at this point in my life—when I'm fifty-three years old and have lived most of my life in the United States but never left my connection to the island behind—there was a story in my poetry finally and it had to do with coming from Spanish, beginning Spanish on the island where I was born and my parents were married, to my present situation, which is I live in Georgia, I consider this my home; I have a family and a love story here.

I think all human life is a love story, not necessarily a romantic story but one of connections you make along the way. Mine began in Spanish and is now in English, but it goes back to Spanish. What I wanted was [for] the poems to reflect that, to have a sense of continuation. So that's where the idea came from: the love story has to do with the fact that I have a very strong narrative impulse. Even when I'm writing poetry, I'm thinking in terms of how does this affect my narrative. How can I plug it into a narrative? I don't think in manipulative terms, but that's how my brain works. I had originally thought that the title poem, "El Amor: A Story Beginning in Spanish," would be the first, but I thought, in a way that announces that the story has closure, so I moved it to the end because that poem says a story can begin anywhere in any language at any time. I wanted it to remain open—that the story is always happening. It's an *Ars Poetica*.

SHEA: When you republish a poem as part of a book, do you revise it? Do you feel that's cricket—or is the poem frozen in the moment of time when you first published it?

COFER: Absolutely I revise. The poem is mine, and it belongs to the journal when it first appears. I think it was Auden who said a poem is never really finished; we just abandon it at some point. To me, poetry is an attempt at the perfection of language, which is of course impossible in human terms. But every time I look at a line, I ask myself, can it be made better? Coleridge said a good poem is "the best words in the best order." That sounds simple, but what is "best"? Many of the poems that are now in this book appear from slightly changed to dramatically changed, because I have changed and learned a few things.

SHEA: There are several Penelope poems in the section From a Sailor's Wife's Journal. How did they come about?

COFER: The actual genesis of those and some on the Bible as well came from my having to teach both parts of world literature when I was first starting out. I had to read these texts very carefully, and I started feeling cheated out of the voice of Penelope. I think her story was more interesting than Odysseus's. His was episodic—then I did this, then I had an affair with Calypso, which is all very fascinating, but Penelope's personal life interested me.

I'm also interested because Penelope's a sailor's wife—which was my mother. I don't think people need to know that, but any woman will recognize Penelope's anguish and her need to fly off and to have a life outside of the palace. I started a series of these poems, and the ones in the book are only a small portion because I found myself weaving and unweaving, as Penelope was doing, trying to get her out of the house.

SHEA: They seem more romantic than many I've read (such as Carol Ann Duffy's "Penelope") which are more feminist talking-back readings. Yours seem dreamy almost, a saddened Penelope but one still longing for her beloved Odysseus.

COFER: I don't see them as romantic. I see the first poem, "Dear Odysseus," as a woman in love yearning to go with her man and for her man to return. But I see the series as a progressive separation. She remembers him as this romantic hero who doesn't want to stay on the farm. She also sees the carolers and partiers coming home from a pagan ritual and having made love and drunk wine—and there's a yearning there. So I saw Penelope's separation not as "Oh, I'm liberated now; I think I'll raise hell." I saw it as an intellectual and emotional coming to terms with her independence, so the poems are meditative in that way. I see my Penelope coming to liberation but not getting up on a stage and announcing, "I'm a liberated woman now." That's not how it happened to my mother or a lot of women; first it's emotional. I tried to infuse those poems with images of flight and freedom that she's considering.

SHEA: Your Penelope is also very attuned to her own sexuality.

COFER: That reflects my kind of feminism, which doesn't reject the romance of the flesh, doesn't reject a woman admitting that she's weak in love but strong in her mind. Maybe that's my Latina-ness, but I've never felt the need to grandstand my liberation. It's internal, and I try to live life as a free woman, but that doesn't eliminate the possibility of being connected to another human being through passion and sexuality.

SHEA: For some time, I've wanted to ask you about the hibiscus. Obviously, this flower means a great deal to you (it's a kind of hallmark of your Web site)—what's your connection to this "ephemeral flower . . . A shrouded female form. / A beauty in her own time? / Lost gospel in a scroll, too small to read"—the description in the poem "I Give You This Hibiscus"?

COFER: You're getting the inside story in a way: this was a gift I made for my daughter. The poem was dedicated to Tanya. The hibiscus represents my background. It was the first flower I became aware of as a child because it was all over the island. In *Silent Dancing*, I talk about how the hibiscus was everywhere. As little girls, my cousins and I used to play with them—we rolled them up and pretended they were cigarettes, we put them in our hair; they represented the island. But in this poem, there's the one thing I didn't think about as a child—how brief the hibiscus's life was, how beautiful it was in full bloom, and how suddenly it wrapped itself into a little shroud. It allows me a moment of meditation about a woman's beauty in her life.

The reader doesn't need to know this, but this was a time when my daughter—who is a mathematician and a wonderful gardener and cook (unlike her mother)—was feeling depressed. I took her this hibiscus that I had bought, and before I gave it to her, I looked up information about it. That description yielded the images in the poem. It's a sort of carpe diem poem, not an original theme, but it says to enjoy the flower, understand it is beautiful and also has practical uses, but it is suddenly gone.

SHEA: This collection opens with a quote from Denise Levertov: "You invaded my country by accident, / not knowing you had crossed the border." Is she one of your favorites?

COFER: When I was an undergraduate in college, she was one of the few female poets I found in anthologies. She wrote about the Vietnam War, but I thought that the line—"you invaded my country"—could be taken in any number of ways. I wanted an ironic reversal on immigration: I have not invaded your country; this culture has invaded my country and my internal country too. I found her words particularly appropriate for what I was trying to do.

SHEA: I want to turn to *Call Me María* now. In your letter to the reader that you did for the publisher, you quote [Constantine] Cavafy's poem "Ithaka"—more Homer. You seem to have a real connection to *The Odyssey*.

COFER: I can't help but be an English teacher, and this seminal story of loss, separation, and beauty mirrors everything I have known in my life: my father was a veteran of every war since Korea until he died, my mother lived a life of exile and waiting, we were influenced by history because my father was always involved in it, we were brought to the U.S. but lived in a bubble of culture. *The Odyssey* has been a key to understanding the recurrent nature of certain events. In this ancient text, Homer brought in the idea of the family waiting for the warrior, and it gave me a framework for thinking about my life. In fact, I recently wrote a chapter for a high school textbook on the work of Cavafy because I love his work. Those lines—"As you set out for Ithaka / hope the voyage is a long one, / full of adventure, full of discovery"—have meant a lot to me because my father's journey was long and full of adventure but not happy, and I wanted something different for me and my child.

SHEA: This book multigenres multigenres with the poetry, narratives, letters—and you call it "a novel in letters, poems, and prose." How does something like that start—with a poem? When did you know this "novel" would be multigenre?

COFER: When I started thinking about this book, I was doing a lot of travel and trying to keep a notebook, asking myself, "Who is the character?" I often do this: in order to think about a character or a situation, I will start a poem about it. To me, poetry is a door to a place that may be lost in my brain. When I am writing a poem, I actually have to set an alarm because—and this is not mystical, it's psychological—I enter a place where I am trying to do what psychologists do in deep analysis. Some of the poems toward the end of the book came to me first, and that's how I started entering María's brain or personality.

At some point, I had all these pieces, which I sent to my editor and said, "I think I'm going to try writing this book in sections because this is how it's coming to me." She liked some of the pieces so much that I started thinking of María as someone watching the world, collecting, and trying to make a collage of some sort appear. As soon as I knew she lived in a basement apartment and was watching the world go by through the top half of her window and she would hear voices and was separated from the world, I started thinking in terms of what impressions she was gathering. So I had her writing things about her teachers, about her friends, the smell of cologne. She comforts herself in her initial loneliness by trying to construct the world. The more I wrote and sent to my editor, the more she liked the idea of allowing María's voice to emerge.

SHEA: So much of your work is about writing, literally and figuratively writing oneself into the world, but this one is quite deliberately so. Again, I am quoting your letter to your reader: "I wanted María to learn to give meaning to her journey by becoming a recorder of experience, that is, a writer." Can you talk a little about why you did that—because it seems to me that making her so specifically a writer might narrow the audience that feels connected to her.

COFER: I hope that hasn't happened. When I go to schools, often with immigrant students, the last thing they think about is the writer, but what they see is that she is a girl desperately trying to find a place and to find language. She just happens to use writing. They mainly talk about her relationships with Whoopi and Uma, her *abuela*, her parents. The fact that she is a writer is coincidental to many of these kids. They seem to think of the writing as a way she has found to integrate herself into the barrio.

SHEA: As you wrote those poems that are about grammar and syntax—technical elements of language—"English Declaration: I Am the Subject of the Sentence" or "English: I Am the Simple Sentence"—did you have in mind kind of a didactic purpose for your young audience?

COFER: Not at all—I'm completely against didacticism in art. I think any lessons in art should be subliminal and playful. I thought of this as simply a frame for where the kids go during the day. They have to put up with teachers telling them about grammar and sentences—I tried to imagine myself, and I was nerdish—so María takes these boring exercises she was given to do and makes them into poems.

SHEA: I have to say that this one is a valentine to teachers—and most of all to your husband, I think (though he's a math teacher).

COFER: The whole book is dedicated to my husband. The students call him Mr. C. He teaches math, and I wrote that poem "Math Class: Sharing the Pie" completely about him. Talk about an idealist! People think that because I'm the poet that I'm the idealist, but it's not true. My husband teaches for almost no money in a high-poverty school in rural Georgia, spending ten- or twelve-hour days trying to convince kids math is beautiful. One thing I did that was kind of strange was that I imagined my husband in a school in New York, yearning for Georgia. I wanted María to see that her nostalgia and loneliness was not just because she was a Puerto Rican girl, but there could be this white guy from the South also yearning for a completely different landscape and also feeling alienated and lost. Mr. Golden is a poet—who tells the kids he has learned math by counting birds. So this is a tribute to the heroes of the classroom, the ones who really do care.

SHEA: María has to be one of your favorite characters—such an exceptional person you've created. Is she?

COFER: I like her because even though she is a bookworm, she is completely involved in life. María and I are only similar in a few ways—her parents are not mine—but what I like about her is that she chooses to be with the parent who needs her the most. She doesn't choose the easy life, but she loves her father despite the fact that he's a mess. She despairs at his womanizing and drinking, but she is still his collaborator. I like her not so much because she's a bookworm like me but because she jumps into life and doesn't take the easy way out.

SHEA: Comparisons to Sandra Cisneros's *House on Mango Street* seem inevitable. Were you inspired by Esperanza and her quest, or do you see these more as parallel tracks?

COFER: I considered that, but I think *María* is different. The form [of vignettes, poetry, and prose] may be similar, but I've done this before in *The Latin Deli*. Sandra did a fabulous job and no one can imitate *The House on Mango Street*, so I knew the comparisons would be made because we're both Latina. But I don't think Esperanza and María are the same. Do you?

SHEA: Both are writers. Both seem to be finding an individual voice to speak for the community.

COFER: But María stays. She's not just interested in telling the stories. She wants to find a voice for herself. Esperanza is gaining power so she can leave and tell the stories, but María chooses to stay in the barrio. But any comparison to Sandra I consider a great compliment.

SHEA: Also in that letter to the reader you wrote, "Language wins you friendship and buys you freedom." I doubt that the Spanish or Spanglish always wins you friends. Doesn't it sometimes distance readers?

COFER: This may sound harsh, but I am not thinking of the reader when I'm writing: I'm thinking of the story. If it requires Spanish or Spanglish, that's what I put in, mainly because I think of reading literary works as work, not simply entertainment. When I was trying to become an English teacher and find an identity for myself, I read everything I was told to read. The greatest works often contain many other languages—[various languages in] *The Waste Land* [by T. S. Eliot], Italian with [Ezra] Pound, French with many people. I just assumed if I couldn't grasp the meaning in context, the work was important enough and we were interested enough that we would go find a dictionary and look things up. So, in order to create the world that María lives in, I could not write all Standard English. I try to use my art and craft to provide context, but I expect my reader to find a way to understand the culture I'm writing about.

SHEA: In another interview, you said that you're not a political writer "in that I never take an issue and write a story about it . . . . [T]he politics are background noise." Yet the stand you implicitly take about language seems very political.

COFER: Is nobody going to read Mark Twain because of the dialect? Or Zora Neale Hurston? I claim the right as a writer to have my characters speak credibly in their chosen form. I may not be a political writer, but it doesn't mean I'm not a political person. My politics are infused in my work.

SHEA: Politics are certainly infused in *The Meaning of Consuelo*, and I wonder if Consuelo is a character you couldn't have written until now. Is she someone you wouldn't have been able to get inside of even, say, ten years ago?

COFER: That's very insightful. Consuelo in many of the reviews is called "grim" or kind of dark. But this is a story I had to write when I felt I had enough distance and compassion for my culture. I love all the celebratory aspects of the Puerto Rican culture, and I feel so grateful to have come from a culture that has yielded so much for my work. But there are also things that bother me, such as the homophobia and how the Catholic Church has conspired to maintain this sense of the woman as servant, the suffering one. In this book, I wanted a girl growing up in a time when she saw options and had to make painful choices to define herself.

That's why I called it *The Meaning of Consuelo. Consuelo* means "comfort." She was born and raised to play a part and at some point she has to define what Consuelo means, that she will be Consuelo, her own comfort. I had to know something first—that takes living—it could not have been my first novel.

SHEA: This is your first real mainstream press book—Farrar, Straus and Giroux. Has this made a big difference? I know you've talked about appreciating the support of smaller presses yet feeling frustrated by the lack of resources for both ensuring a first-rate presentation and promoting the book. Is this a breakthrough? Why do you think FSG was interested in it—because of your reputation and prizes or the story itself?

COFER: I haven't moved into the mainstream. I'm not a bestselling author in terms of huge numbers; my great luck is that my work is used extensively in high school and college textbooks. I think Farrar, Straus took a chance on me. I've been very aware that I have a public, but it doesn't have to do with the masses, just a faithful, loyal following.

There's not a linear progression of success, as though I started out with a little press and worked up to FSG. I am thrilled to be published with them, and Beacon Press has done a fabulous job with the paperback. But every book is different. Recently, University of Georgia Press has done something very courageous. They've commissioned a translation of *Woman in Front of the Sun*, and it's coming out in Spanish. Poetry is almost impossible to place. University of Georgia Press has been loyal and kept my books in print no matter what the numbers, so I give them the poetry. If I write another novel, my agent will send it around, and it will find a publisher.

SHEA: You've written about your grandmother's influence on you through her storytelling and much more (though she was not formally educated). You pointed out in an interview [Elliott Gordon] that she "belonged to a generation of women who did not need political rhetoric to establish themselves as matriarchs and liberated women." What exactly did you mean?

COFER: I think that part of my stance as a feminist comes from my grandmother as well as my mother. Mama (my name for her; Mami is my mother) never doubted her own power for one minute, yet she was maternal, nurturing, and as feminine as any woman I've ever known. She did not feel that one negated the other. She empowered herself internally. She didn't have to go around saying, "I am woman, hear me roar"; she just roared! She was a great model because she took action, she was a great problem solver, and yet she never talked about her philosophy of feminism. I just knew that all of her actions were based on her ethical system. I watched her be powerful without giving up the things she wanted to have. I've said that I knew I wanted my art but I didn't want to give up being a wife and mother to have it. So many women of my generation at some point in their lives came to believe that it was not possible to have a family and be liberated as a feminist—an early way of looking at things. If someone asked my grandmother who wears the pants in the family, she'd say, "Well, your grandfather does, but why would I need to wear pants? I have the power."

SHEA: When asked where you see literature going in the U.S. in the next two decades—essentially another generation—you predicted that "a new generation of people who are multiracial and multiethnic[,] . . . people who speak standard English, who have gone through the educational process but come from a multitude of cultures, will be creating a literature that will represent the true diversity of this country, not just pockets" [Sandra Lopez]. I think about your grandmother here, but aren't you also describing María and Consuelo?

COFER: Isn't that funny—it takes you to tell me what I think! When I created María and Consuelo, I was thinking not of myself, but, particularly with María, I am thinking of someone who embraces a multitude of tongues and who chooses to speak Standard English when it is necessary in the same way African Americans speak one dialect in the home but understand that when they're on Wall Street, they speak the language of the mainstream. So, right now in my honors undergraduate writing class, I have a girl from Egypt and another from Greece. They're writing stories about leaving their countries and coming to Atlanta, and I think how wonderful if one of these girls becomes a writer—a southern writer.

SHEA: When I saw you last October, you commented, "Young people—my students—are my daily news. If I did not have these encounters, I would live my life more and more internally." Could you talk about that—and could it possibly be true that though gregarious, you are, in fact, more inclined toward being an introvert than [an] extrovert?

COFER: Actually, yes, gregarious is my public persona. When I am not traveling or teaching, I'm usually very alone in what my husband calls the cave or the dungeon. I keep the drapes drawn and everything quiet. I have always had a need for solitude because I live in my mind. I love a day when I don't have to do what I do today—meet students, go to a meeting, a dinner. I will enjoy every minute of this because it's how I absorb life, but then tomorrow I will enjoy staying in my pajamas and working alone in my basement with only one light on. I'm afraid if I didn't have these requirements of students waiting for me, I would more and more live in my mind because that's where my imagination resides. I understand the need for both, which is why I choose to have a family and to teach.

SHEA: I've heard you say many times that you carved out writing time for yourself by reserving 5 to 7 a.m. each day, starting when you had a young daughter. Do you still do that? Do you write every day?

COFER: I still do mainly because I've trained myself. People who run or do one thing obsessively or compulsively at a certain hour find that it becomes a need. I find that my best work comes when I have not spoken to anyone yet, when I've just been asleep the whole night, before I can easily move into this realm right from dreams. It doesn't always end at 7 now because I have more leisure, but I find that about three hours is all I can do.

SHEA: I love seeing the eclecticism of your influences just by reading the epigraphs and introductions to your books: Pablo Neruda, Denise Levertov, Virginia Woolf, May Sarton, W. S. Merwin . . . across time and culture. You must be a voracious reader. . . .

COFER: Out of need and pleasure. One of the things I've been doing lately is taking the writers that I love and reading them from beginning to end. I did that with Flannery O'Connor last summer—all letters, stories, books. I just got everything of [Vladimir] Nabokov to read, but I haven't started yet. But the other thing is that I am on endless comp [comprehensive exam] committees. Writers are not like scholars, because they put together weird lists of what they want to be examined on. I just finished one that made me reread Aristotle's *Poetics*! I may have read these things a long time ago, but once again my students keep me reading far and wide.

SHEA: But another influence—or influences—is Alice Walker and Flannery O'Connor, and you know that one of my very favorite pieces of yours is "In Search of Our Mentors' Gardens," where you talk about them. It seems that you're able to take in so many different approaches and influences, even styles, and appreciate them for one thing or another without judging them.

COFER: This is the thing I tell my graduate students. Everybody feels that they have to write out [of] their own experience and feelings, but the master works of literature have been written when one enters another consciousness—even that of a giant cockroach! I tell them, if you're an African American and reading only African American writers, all you are seeing are things you need to know for yourself as a human being but not as an artist. An artist has to take in *everything*. One of the things I do when I'm teaching a poetry seminar is have my poor graduate assistant go to the library and find every poetry anthology from every poetry ghetto—like Lesbian Poetry Writers of the 1950s or Puerto Ricans Angry at the World—along with the *Norton Anthology* and others, and tell them they must read at least one book per week *out of themselves*. I say, "Does it matter if that poem gives you chills? Does it matter that this guy is a white guy in Vermont?" One of the things I believe in—and maybe I'm sounding political now, but I am a dictator in class—is that people have been taught that they can only think in terms of themselves and write in those terms. That is so wrong. I have found the greatest life lessons in the lives of people I think are reprehensible. I dislike the way James Dickey lived his life, especially the way he treated women, but I still cry when I read some of his poems. So one has to separate prejudice from art. And I have to practice what I preach, so I read people on my students' reading lists whom I wouldn't normally turn to, and often I learn even more about myself.

SHEA: Virginia Woolf certainly isn't inimical to your belief system, though she lived a very different life and came from a different background and time, yet you've written about what a profound influence she's had on you.

COFER: Models are a gift, but you have to discover what you need, and with her, I found an intelligent woman's voice saying, "Dig in your own backyard. You have treasures. Go back into your memory. Follow the track left by some emotions to your moments of being."

SHEA: I want to follow up on a wonderful point you made in an interview, when you talked about the reading and [the] writing being separate activities (you were explaining why you would not choose to read aloud certain of your works). You referred to "the eloquent silence between the writer and the reader" [Sandra Lopez]. What is that "eloquent silence"?

COFER: When I'm reading a story in complete solitude, there is this voice in my head implanting invaluable lessons. So there's a silence in a mystical yet biologically understandable way— passing information from an object in your hand into your most important condition as a human being, your unconscious mind. So the eloquent silence is between the text, writer, and reader—even if the writer is hundreds of years ago. Reading is probably the most important thing I do for myself.

SHEA: I read somewhere that you're working on a novel with an old woman as the protagonist?

COFER: I never finished that. I started some time ago about an old woman who used to be a dancer and was in Miami. But I realized I didn't know enough about this woman. I still think about her. . . . Perhaps some day. I've written so much in the voice of a young person that I definitely want to turn that around.

SHEA: What are you working on now?

COFER: Because I just finished three books in two years and collaborated on this translation, I'm now just planning. I have about fifty pages of notes toward a novel but don't want to talk about it because I don't know if it will happen.

SHEA: But you're always writing poetry, right—what you've called "the ultimate discipline"?

COFER: I work on poems all the time. I have several new ones, but they're not ready to send out. I'm in the gathering stage right now with notes all over my table.

6 More Cofer

■ ■

Judith Ortiz Cofer is an excellent subject for author study in your classroom or for student research projects. To facilitate your and your students' search for materials, here are some of the resources available in bookstores, libraries, and online.

Some Other Books by Judith Ortiz Cofer

Call Me María. New York: Orchard Books, 2004.

In this coming-of-age story told through poems, letters, and prose, the narrator María explores what it means to live in two worlds and to find comfort in words and new friends.

An Island Like You: Stories of the Barrio. New York: Puffin Books, 1995.

Winner of the Américas Book Award for Children's and Young Adult Literature, a *School Library Journal* Best Book of the Year, an ALA Quick Picks for Reluctant Young Adult Readers selection, and an NCTE Notable Children's Book in the English Language Arts, this collection of stories gives voice to immigrant kids torn between their Puerto Rican families and pursuit of the American dream.

The Latin Deli: Telling the Lives of Barrio Women. New York: W. W. Norton, 1995.

This collection of fiction, poetry, and essays has won the Anisfield-Wolf Book Award for "contributing to the rich diversity of human cultures." It is a celebration of the immigrant experience and the challenges of redefining oneself in the United States.

The Meaning of Consuelo. Boston: Beacon Press, 2003.

Winner of the Américas Book Award, this novel tells the story of a brave, serious young woman struggling to come to terms with the roles she must play within her family and in the larger world.

Riding Low on the Streets of Gold: Latino Literature for Young Adults. Houston: Piñata Books. 2003.

Judith Ortiz Cofer edited this collection of stories and poems for young readers, many by writers whose work has yet to be widely distributed. Most of the stories and poems are told in the voices of teenagers going through the difficult transition to adulthood.

Silent Dancing: A Partial Remembrance of a Puerto Rican Childhood. Houston: Arte Público Press, 1990.

This personal narrative describes Cofer's experiences growing up bilingual and bicultural that led to her becoming an artist and writer. The book was awarded the 1991 PEN/Martha Albrand Special Citation for Nonfiction and selected for the New York Public Library's Books for the Teen Age list.

Woman in Front of the Sun: On Becoming a Writer. Athens: University of Georgia Press, 2000.

This collection of folklore, essays, and poems offers insight into the factors contributing to Cofer's emergence as a writer. It explores her love of words and books, which readers will find inspirational.

The Year of Our Revolution: New and Selected Stories and Poems. Houston: Arte Público Press, 1998.

In the season of her rebellion and maturation, Mary Ellen/María Elenita grapples with the disconnection between her dreams and the world around her. The vignettes in this collection are both charming and bittersweet.

Published Essays and Reviews

- Review of *Call Me María* by Lauren Adams. *Horn Book Magazine* 81 (Jan./Feb. 2005): 90.

- Review of *Call Me María*. *Library Journal* 50 (Nov. 2004): 138.

- Review of *Call Me María*. *Kirkus Reviews* 72 (15 Oct. 2004): 1003.

- Review of *The Meaning of Consuelo* by Emily Spicer. *San Antonio Express-News*, 4 January 2004.

- Review of *The Meaning of Consuelo* by Patricia Maldonado. *Hispanic Magazine* 16 (2003): 58.

- Review of *The Meaning of Consuelo* by Malena Watrous. *The San Francisco Chronicle*, 21 December 2003: M5.

- "For University of Georgia Professor Judith Ortiz Cofer, Writing Is Art" by Wayne Ford. Interview and discussion of *The Meaning of Consuelo*. *The Athens Banner-Herald*, 14 December 2003.

- Review of *The Meaning of Consuelo* by Emiliana Sandoval. *Detroit Free Press*, 9 November 2003.

- "Cold/Hot, English/Spanish: The Puerto Rican American Divide in Judith Ortiz Cofer's *Silent Dancing*" by Teresa Derrickson. *MELUS* 28 (2003): 121–37.

Judith Ortiz Cofer on the Web

Note: Every effort has been made to provide current URLs, but because of the rapidly changing nature of the Web, some sites and addresses may no longer be accessible.

- Judith Ortiz Cofer homepage: http://www.english.uga.edu/~jcofer/home.html

- The New Georgia Encyclopedia. Judith Ortiz Cofer entry: http://www.georgiaencyclopedia.org/nge/Article.jsp?id=h-488
- The Chelsea Forum. Judith Ortiz Cofer entry: http://www.chelseaforum.com/speakers/Cofer.htm
- The Literary Encyclopedia. Judith Ortiz Cofer entry: http://www.litencyc.com/php/speople.php?rec=true&UID=4978
- Judith Ortiz Cofer: Articles, Reviews, Interviews, and Dissertations about Her Work: http://www.english.uga.edu/~jcofer/Judith%20articles%20about.html
- Masterpiece Theater "Almost a Woman" Project. Judith Ortiz Cofer page: http://www.pbs.org/wgbh/masterpiece/americancollection/woman/ei_poetry_cofer.html

Chronology of Judith Ortiz Cofer's Life

■ ■

1952   Born on February 24 in Hormigueros, Puerto Rico.

1955   Family moves to Paterson, New Jersey, and fre-
        quently returns to Puerto Rico during father's Navy
        tours of duty.

1968   Family moves to Augusta, Georgia.

1970   Graduates from high school. Enrolls at Augusta
        College, Augusta, Georgia.

1971   Marries John Cofer.

1973   Daughter, Tanya Cofer, is born.

1974   Cofer graduates from Augusta College.

1977   Cofer writes a master's thesis titled "Lillian Hellman's
        Southern Plays" and is awarded an English Speaking
        Union Graduate Fellowship to Oxford University,
        England. She earns her MA from Florida Atlantic
        University.

1978–81   Cofer works as an instructor at Broward Community College.

1981   Awarded a scholarship from the Bread Loaf Writers' Conference

1981–84   Cofer employed as a lecturer at the University of Miami.

1986   Cofer's first poetry chapbook, *Peregrina*, is published by Riverstone Press and wins first place in the Riverstone International Chapbook Competition, 1985.

1987   *Terms of Survival* published by Arte Público Press.

1989   Cofer's first novel, *The Line of the Sun*, is published by University of Georgia Press, and Cofer is awarded a National Endowment for the Arts Fellowship in Poetry.

1990   *Silent Dancing: A Partial Remembrance of a Puerto Rican Childhood* is published by Arte Público Press. The book receives a PEN/Martha Albrand Special Citation in nonfiction. Cofer wins a Pushcart Prize in nonfiction.

1991   "Silent Dancing" chosen by Joyce Carol Oates for inclusion in *The Best American Essays*.

1993   *The Latin Deli: Telling the Lives of Barrio Women*
        published by University of Georgia Press. It is
        awarded the Anisfield-Wolf Book Award in Race
        Relations. The story "Nada" is selected for the
        O'Henry Prize anthology.

1995   Norton publishes paperback edition of *The Latin
        Deli. Reaching for the Mainland and Selected New
        Poems* published by Bilingual Press

1998   *The Year of Our Revolution: New and Selected Stories
        and Poems* published by Piñata Books.

1999   Cofer is awarded a Rockefeller Foundation residency
        at the Conference Center in Bellagio, Italy. Awarded
        the title of Franklin Professor of English and Creative
        Writing by the University of Georgia.

2000   *Woman in Front of the Sun: On Becoming a Writer*
        published by University of Georgia Press.

2001   Penguin USA (Puffin Books) publishes a paperback
        edition of *The Year of Our Revolution*. Cofer selected
        as the Gertrude and Harold S. Vanderbilt Visiting
        Writer in Residence at Vanderbilt University.

2002   Awarded *Prairie Schooner* Reader's Choice Awards for
        two poems in the fall issue of *Prairie Schooner*.

2003   *The Meaning of Consuelo* published by Farrar, Straus
        and Giroux. It wins the Américas Book Award. Cofer
        is awarded the Love of Learning Award, Honor
        Society of Phi Kappa Phi, University of Georgia
        Chapter, Athens.

2004   *Call Me María* published by Scholastic (Orchard
        Books). It is one of two Honor Books in the
        Américas Award.

2005   *A Love Story Beginning in Spanish: Poems* is published
        by University of Georgia Press.

Works Cited

ACHIEVE, INC. 2005. *Rising to the Challenge: Are High School Graduates Prepared for College and Work?* Washington, DC: Achieve, Inc. <http ://www.achieve.org/dstore.nsf/Lookup/pollreport/$file/poll report.pdf>.

AMERICAN DIPLOMA PROJECT. 2004. *Ready or Not: Creating a High School Diploma That Counts.* Washington, DC: Achieve. <http://www. achieve.org/dstore.nsf/Lookup/ADPreport/$file/ADPreport.pdf>.

AUSTEN, JANE. 2003. *Pride and Prejudice.* New York: Penguin Books.

CALIFORNIA DEPARTMENT OF EDUCATION. 1997. *California Reading/Language Arts Standards.* Sacramento: California Department of Education.

COFER, JUDITH ORTIZ. 2004. *Call Me María.* New York: Orchard Books.

———. 1995. *An Island Like You: Stories of the Barrio.* New York: Puffin Books.

———. 1995. *The Latin Deli: Telling the Lives of Barrio Women.* New York: W. W. Norton.

———. 2003. *The Meaning of Consuelo.* Boston: Beacon Press.

———. 1992. "My Grandfather's Hat." *The Bilingual Review* 17.2: 161.

———. 2003. *Riding Low on the Streets of Gold: Latino Literature for Young Adults.* Houston: Piñata Books.

———. 1990. *Silent Dancing: A Partial Remembrance of a Puerto Rican Childhood.* Houston: Arte Público Press.

———. 2000. *Woman in Front of the Sun: On Becoming a Writer.* Athens: University of Georgia Press.

————. 1998. *The Year of Our Revolution: New and Selected Stories and Poems.* Houston: Piñata Books.

FLETCHER, RALPH, AND JOANN PORTALUPI. 1998. *Craft Lessons: Teaching Writing K–8.* York, ME: Stenhouse.

GARDNER, JOHN. 1991. *The Art of Fiction: Notes on Craft for Young Writers.* New York: Vintage Books.

NATIONAL ENDOWMENT FOR THE ARTS. 2004. *Reading at Risk: A Survey of Literary Reading in America.* Research Division Report #46. Washington, DC: National Endowment for the Arts. <http://www.nea.gov/pub/ReadingAtRisk.pdf>.

NUSSBAUM, MARTHA C. 1995. *Poetic Justice: The Literary Imagination and Public Life.* Boston: Beacon Press.

POE, EDGAR ALLAN. 1846. "The Philosophy of Composition." *Graham's Magazine* (April): 163–67.

SALINGER, J. D. 1991. *The Catcher in the Rye.* Boston: Little, Brown.

VYGOTSKY, L. S. 1962. *Thought and Language.* Ed. and Trans. E. Hanfmann and G. Vakar. Cambridge, MA: MIT Press.

Author

Carol Jago teaches English and is department chair at Santa Monica High School in Santa Monica, California. She also directs the California Reading and Literature Project at UCLA and edits the California Association of Teachers of English quarterly journal, *California English*. Jago has written a weekly education column for the *Los Angeles Times*, and her essays have appeared in *English Journal*, *Language Arts*, and *NEA Today*, as well as in other newspapers across the nation. She is currently a content advisor for the College Board's AP Central Advanced Placement Literature Web site. She served as director of the National Council of Teachers of English Commission on Literature and as a member of NCTE's Secondary Section. NCTE has published her three volumes in the NCTE High School Literature series: *Nikki Giovanni in the Classroom*, *Alice Walker in the Classroom*, and *Sandra Cisneros in the Classroom*. Other publications include *With Rigor for All: Teaching the Classics to Contemporary Students* (2000), *Beyond Standards: Excellence in the High School English Classroom* (2001), *Cohesive Writing: Why Concept Is Not Enough* (2002), *Classics in the Classroom: Designing Accessible Literature Lessons* (2004) (published with accompanying video), and *Papers, Papers, Papers: An English*

Teacher's Survival Guide (2005). Jago serves on the planning committee for the 2009 NAEP Reading Framework and the 2011 NAEP Writing Framework.

This book was composed by Electronic Imaging in Berkeley,
Interstate, and Old Style 7.

The typefaces used on the cover include Trebuchet MS
and Zurich Ex BT.

The book was printed on 50-lb. Williamsburg Offset paper
by Versa Press, Inc.